THE G.I. SERIES

Hell on Wheels
The Men of the U.S. Armored Forces, 1918 to the Present

A tank helps members of the 44th Infantry Division cross the Danube with dry feet. The two tank crewmen are distinguishable from the infantrymen by their winter combat jackets and wool-knit caps. The crew are carrying additional personal equipment in boxes secured to the rear of the tank.

THE G.I. SERIES

THE ILLUSTRATED HISTORY OF THE AMERICAN
SOLDIER, HIS UNIFORM AND HIS EQUIPMENT

Hell on Wheels

The Men of the U.S. Armored Forces, 1918 to the Present

Christopher J. Anderson

Greenhill Books
LONDON

Stackpole Books
PENNSYLVANIA

Greenhill Books

Hell on Wheels first published 1999
by Greenhill Books, Lionel Leventhal Limited, Park
House, 1 Russell Gardens, London NW11 9NN
www.greenhillbooks.com
and
Stackpole Books, 5067 Ritter Road, Mechanicsburg,
PA 17055, USA

British Library Cataloguing in Publication Data
Anderson, Christopher J.
Hell on Wheels : the Men of the U.S. Armored Forces,
1918 to the Present. - (The G.I. series : the illustrated
history of the American soldier, his uniform and his
equipment ; v. 17)
1. United States - Armed Forces - Armored troops -
Pictorial works
I. Title
358.1'0973

ISBN 1-85367-378-1
*Library of Congress Cataloging-in-Publication
Data available*

Acknowledgements
I would like to thank Dr John Langellier for his help
in the preparation of this book.

All the images in this book are U.S. Army pho-
tographs, unless credited otherwise.

Design and layout by David Gibbons and
Anthony A. Evans, DAG Publications Ltd
Edited by Proof Positive
Printed in Hong Kong

HELL ON WHEELS
THE MEN OF THE U.S. ARMORED FORCES, 1918 TO THE PRESENT

At 5a.m. on 12 September 1918, Lieutenant Colonel George S. Patton led the attack of the United States Army's 344th and 345th Tank Battalions during the first day of the St Mihiel offensive. The attack was the fruition of nine months of effort on the part of pioneering American officers like Patton and Colonel S.D. Rockenbach, the latter of whom had been named American Tank Corps' first commander on 26 January 1918. With no precedent to guide their efforts, they laid the foundation for the armored forces. As Patton wrote when ordered to report on the French armored forces, 'The job I have tentatively possessed myself of is huge, for everything must be created and there is nothing to start with.'

Not only was there no doctrine, there were no vehicles. Despite the industrial might of the United States, at the time of its entry into World War I its army was so small and inadequate to the task of fighting in a major European conflict that the bulk of its heavy equipment, including artillery, aircraft and tanks, was provided by its allies. The primary tank used by the American army in France was the French-built Renault FT17, a light, two-man tank armed with a 37 mm cannon and with a road speed of 5.5 miles per hour. Additional American tank units were equipped with the British Mark V heavy tank, a silhouette of which was later adopted as the first insignia of the American Tank Corps. While American industry produced copies of the French and British tanks under license, none of the American-built tanks arrived in France before the armistice. The early armored officers familiarized themselves with their new vehicles through learning from their allies.

It is no coincidence that after observing the French, Patton, a cavalry officer, wrote a doctrine for the Tank Corps that emphasized speed and mobility. Although it seemed unlikely, the ponderous and lightly armored French Renault tanks that the Americans were first equipped with would become the inheritor of the American army's long mounted tradition. In describing what he intended the role of the armored forces to be, Patton wrote, 'If resistance is broken and the line pierced the tank must and will assume the role of pursuit cavalry and "ride the enemy to death".' The organization that Patton proposed, and the army adopted, was for tank battalions of seventy-seven tanks to support infantry advances by deployment in large enough numbers to breach enemy defensive positions.

Patton embraced the possibilities of armor to break the stalemate of trench warfare, and was determined to see the new branch succeed. While developing the doctrine that the American armored forces would use, Patton also sought a means of instilling the *esprit de corps* that had long been a part of America's mounted tradition. It was Patton, and the other officers of the first tank school at Langres, France, who fostered the idea among America's first armored soldiers that they were members of an élite corps within the army. To foster this sense of pride, Patton instructed his officers to develop an insignia that the men could wear as a distinguishing feature. According to Will G. Robinson, one of Patton's officers, 'I want you officers to devote one evening to something constructive. I want a shoulder insignia. We claim to have the firepower of artillery, the mobility of cavalry and the ability to hold ground of the infantry so whatever you come up with it must have red, yellow, and blue [branch of service colors for the three branches] in it.' The design that Robinson and his roommate Lieutenant Howard came up with was the triangular insignia worn by all armored soldiers to the present day, which Patton paid for out of his own pocket.

All the training and preparation of the early pioneers paid off during the St Mihiel offensive when the armored forces aided the advance of American infantry divisions. Although unable to advance as rapidly as they hoped because of the slowness of their tanks and the broken terrain, the Americans were able to score considerable success against heavily defended German positions. During the remaining two months of the war, American armored forces would continue this record of success.

While much thought had been given to the doctrine and potential of tanks during the war, the innovation that had created the tank did not extend to the uniforms of the men expected to operate them. Armored warfare was so new that very little consideration had been given to the development of specialized clothing and equipment. Although tank crewmen had a distinctive insignia by the end of the war, little else had been developed that would set the armored soldier apart from his compatriots in any other branch.

The American tankers of World War I wore the high-collared model 1912 wool coat, wool breeches, overseas caps and puttees that were standard amongst the doughboys. For added warmth the men were issued with long M1917 wool overcoats, which extended well below the knee. It was quickly realized that they were impractical inside the confines of the tiny Renaults, and Patton ordered them to be cut down to knee length with a belt added to the waist. Even this was found to be quite bulky, and American tankers are often pictured wearing the leather jerkin that was popular amongst British and American infantrymen. For head protection, the crewmen wore the standard dishpan helmet, which was sometimes fitted with a chain-mailed face veil. In addition, some tankers were able to obtain special goggles that protected the eyes. These uniforms continued to be worn after the armistice in 1918.

During the 1920s and 1930s, the army largely forgot the contribution and potential of the tank. In the 1920s, George Patton, fearing that there was no future in tanks, returned to the Cavalry. Even though the Tank Corps disappeared as an independent branch of the army in 1920, some visionary officers like Generals Adna Chaffee and Daniel van Voorhis continued to fight on behalf of the tank.

The neglect of armored warfare continued until events in Europe alerted American military planners to the fact that they might be drawn again into a continental war. As Adolf Hitler's panzers blitzed through Poland, American tank forces, inadequately prepared to fight a major

modern war, trained with World War I er Renault tanks and canvas-covered cars. Militar planners began to consider the need for a mor modern, mobile army.

After the fall of France in 1940, a shocke American Congress began to pour money into it much-neglected armed forces. In July 1940, th War Department issued orders that called for th re-creation of an armored force; in September Patton was appointed as commander of the 2 Armored Division and in October the army' armor school was opened at Fort Knox, Kentucky

In addition to reviving the armored forces a an independent branch of service, the arm finally began to replace World War I era tanks. I late 1941, the M3 medium tank began to reach the newly created armored divisions. Although incapable of performing on a modern battlefield the M3 did allow armored units to train in armored doctrine. In 1942, the M4 Sherman tank named in honor of the famous Union Civil Wa general, came into use. Often criticized for it inability to go toe to toe with its more heavily armed opponents, the M4 was nevertheless an effective and versatile weapon that became the work horse of the Allied war effort. American armored forces were also equipped with the M3 Stuart light reconnaissance tank, named for the Confederate cavalry general, which also saw service throughout the war. The tradition of naming American tanks after famous generals was begun by the British when they received the first lend lease tanks from America.

In conjunction with the introduction of new tanks, the army began to develop the specialized clothing required by tank crews. Before 1940 vehicle crewmen were often forced to improvise specialized uniforms and equipment. In late 1941, the first examples of the winter combat uniform began to reach members of the armored divisions. Better known as the tanker uniform, it consisted of cotton twill jacket, trousers and cap that were lined with blanket-weight material. The jackets, originally intended to be worn only by armored forces, became so popular with G.I.s during the war that they came to be worn by soldiers in every branch of the service. When the weather was too warm for winter uniform, tank crewmen would often wear either the standard wool shirt and trousers, or the herringbone twill (HBT) fatigue coveralls. In 1942, tank crewmen began to receive the armored forces crew helmet. Although it offered no ballistic protection, it protected the tank crewman from the protrusions found inside the cramped quarters of the tank, and would ften be worn with the shell of the standard M1 helmet over it for additional protection.

Equipped with modern weapons and equipment and commanded by dynamic men such as Patton, the armored forces quickly regained the *sprit de corps* that had typified their service in World War I. During the course of the war, the army raised sixteen armored divisions and countless independent brigades and battalions, among the earliest of which was the 2d Armored Division, nicknamed by Patton 'Hell on Wheels'. As he had done in World War I, Patton imbued his men with a fierce pride in their branch of service. The habit among tankers of wearing their divisional patch on their left breast, over their heart, instead of on the left shoulder as was the practice among infantry and airborne divisions, began with the 2d Armored Division.

Armored forces came to be the crucial component of Allied success in the Mediterranean theater in 1942 and 1943, and northwest Europe in 1944–45. In the hands of such leaders as Major Generals John Wood and Robert Grow, American armor was finally able to achieve the decisive breakthroughs and rapid advances in Europe that visionaries like Patton and Chaffee had dreamed of in World War I. Although not as prominent as in Europe, American tanks were utilized in the Pacific where they proved to be an important means of supporting infantry operations against Japanese positions. By the end of the war, armored forces had come to dominate American military thinking. The armored forces' dominant role as the army's mobile force was demonstrated in April 1946, when the War Department announced that the use of horses by the army would largely be eliminated and that the armored and cavalry branches would be merged.

As the Cold War began, the American military continued to develop larger and more potent armored forces and deploy them to Europe as a deterrent to Soviet expansion westward. The American military's attention had become so focused on the belief in a large, conventional, armored war fought in Europe that it was caught off guard in June 1950 when communist North Korean forces, spearheaded by large numbers of Soviet-built T34/85 tanks, invaded South Korea and moved rapidly to drive the few Americans present out of Korea.

As the war escalated, America committed increasing numbers of soldiers to Korea. Although it was not well suited for the deployment of large armored formations, the army did send some armored units there. Sherman tanks were used alongside the heavier Pershing and light Chaffee tanks (named after the commander of the American army in World War I and one of the early armored theorists respectively) that had been developed at the end of World War II. Armor was largely used as mobile artillery or as direct support to infantry units.

In Korea, tankers wore the M1943 universal clothing that had been developed at the end of World War II to replace specialized uniforms. In addition to the M1943 and HBT clothing that had been worn during World War II, tankers wore a variety of parkas and other cold weather gear to survive in the severe Korean winter.

While the army deployed smaller armored formations to Korea, it continued to maintain armored divisions in the United States. As part of the commitment to the North Atlantic Treaty Organization, large numbers of tanks were also deployed to Europe to guard the border between East and West.

Following the Korean cease-fire in 1953, America returned to its deployment of large forces to Europe and its emphasis on heavy armored formations. The army continued with this notion of a massive armored battle being fought in Europe, and much of its armored development was focused in this direction throughout the remainder of the 1950s and into the 1960s. It was during this time that the heavier M48 tanks were introduced to replace the remaining Sherman and Pershing tanks. Tankers continued to wear the uniforms that were being worn by the rest of the army. By the 1950s, these included the cotton sateen uniforms which replaced the earlier HBT fatigue uniforms.

The most significant development in armored uniforms in the period before the Vietnam War was the combat vehicle crewman's helmet, which finally combined the ballistic protection of the steel M1 helmet with the convenience of the armored forces helmet. It was made of nylon and had an integral headset that could be plugged into the vehicle.

Throughout the first half of the 1960s, as America became increasingly involved in combat operations in Vietnam, the army continued to believe that the most likely use of its armored forces would be in Europe. Most armored theorists believed that the jungles and rice paddies of Vietnam were wholly unsuited to the deployment of armored forces. However, in 1965, the situation in southeast Asia had escalated to the point that Military Assistance Command Vietnam (MACV) commander, Lieutenant General William Westmoreland, requested armored support.

The 1st Battalion, 4th Cavalry, was the first army armored unit to arrive in Vietnam, the first armored unit to arrive being Company B of the 3rd Marine Tank Battalion. They were soon followed by the 11th Armored Cavalry Regiment (ACR), which was so successful in supporting infantry operations and guarding convoys along South Vietnam's roadways that other armored units soon followed. Tankers in Vietnam most frequently used M48 and M551 tanks and M113 armored personnel carriers. They wore the jungle fatigue uniform popular with all personnel in Vietnam, together with the combat vehicle crewman's helmet and either the M1952 or M1969 flak vest.

Armored forces continued to be used in penny packets throughout the remainder of the Vietnam War. While small numbers of armored vehicles were used in Vietnam, the army continued to maintain larger formations in Europe. Following the final American withdrawal, the armored forces returned to their primary Cold War mission of deterrence.

After America's withdrawal from Vietnam, the army underwent much soul-searching as to the causes of defeat and its future focus. While some advocated a return to the traditional plan of maintaining a large forward-deployed force in Europe to counter any Soviet threat, there were others who believed that, owing to the increased lethality of the modern battlefield and the experience of the army in Korea and Vietnam, the days of large numbers of tanks fighting a conventional battle on the plains of Europe were over. The idea that the practicality of the tank on the modern battlefield was limited gained further credence during the 1973 Arab–Israeli Yom Kippur War. During this war it was found that large numbers of American-built Israeli tanks were being destroyed by cheap, man-portable Egyptian anti-tank weapons of Soviet design. The notion that an individual infantryman could destroy a tank sent shock waves through the armored establishment and sparked significant developments in armor–infantry integration and tactics, and improved armor design.

Throughout the remaining years of the Cold War, as strategists debated the future role of the tank, improved vehicles and equipment continued to arrive in the American inventory. The M60 tank had replaced the M48 by the 1970s, and itself began to be replaced in the 1980s by the M1 Abrams tank, named after former chief of staff of the army and armored officer Creighton Abrams. As the tanks were improved, so were the uniforms and equipment of the vehicle crewmen. By the 1980s, tankers had a wide variety of specialized clothing and equipment that improved their comfort and effectiveness. Yet, despite all of these improvements, there were still many who believed that the tank's days on the modern battlefield were numbered.

All of that changed on 2 August 1990, after Iraq's president, Saddam Hussein, invaded Kuwait. After seizing control of Kuwait, Hussein began to make threatening gestures toward Saudi Arabia. President George Bush reacted to the increased Iraqi threat with a massive deployment of U.S. forces, including large numbers of M1A Abrams tanks, to Saudi Arabia. On 16 January 1991, after the failure of negotiations designed to oust the Iraqis peacefully from Kuwait, the United States, acting in concert with its thirty-one allies, began air strikes on Iraqi positions. On 24 February, General Norman Schwarzkopf, commander of allied forces in Saudi Arabia, launched the ground war. Part of Schwarzkopf's plan included a massive flanking maneuver of infantry and armored units across the desert. During the next three days, in one of the most decisive military victories in history, allied forces destroyed twenty-nine Iraqi divisions. American armored formations repeatedly mauled Iraqi units.

The overwhelming success of allied forces in the Persian Gulf was achieved largely through the close co-operation of aviation and armored assets. The tankers' performance during the Persian Gulf War continued the long tradition of battlefield success that began in September 1918 and ensured that there would continue to be a place for the tank on a modern battlefield.

Bibliography

Anderson, Christopher J., *Patton's Third Army* (Greenhill Books, 1997).

Anderson, Christopher J., *The U.S. Army Today* (Greenhill Books, 1997).

Blumeson, Martin, *The Patton Papers* (DaCapo Press, 1998).

Gawne, Jonathan, *Over There! The American Soldier in World War I* (Greenhill Books, 1997).

Hogg, Ian V. (ed.), *The American Arsenal: The World War II Official Standard Ordnance Catalog* (Greenhill Books, 1996).

Langellier, John, *The War in Europe: From the Kasserine Pass to Berlin, 1942–1945* (Greenhill Books, 1995, revised edition 1998).

Thompson, Leroy, *The U.S. Army in Vietnam* (David and Charles, 1990).

Top: During training maneuvers in 1942, a tank of the 40th Tank Battalion, 7th Armored Division, receives on-the-spot maintenance from the tank's maintenance section. Mechanics and crewmen are all wearing the M1938 one-piece HBT mechanics' coveralls. Only the technical sergeant resting on the tank's barrel is wearing the armored forces crash helmet. (Ethell Collection)

Above: During Stateside training, a tank from the 11th Tank Battalion, 10th Armored Division, trains with attached armored infantrymen. The unit identification can be seen on the front of the tank. The identification has been painted on to signify division, regiment and company. The triangles after each number were used to signify an armored formation. These designations would have been painted on every vehicle in the unit. (Ethell Collection)

Above: At the end of desert maneuvers, the crew of an M4 Sherman tank prepare to shake the dust off their uniforms. These three men are all wearing the first pattern of HBT coveralls. Breast pockets on later models would have button closures. (Ethell Collection)

Left: Major General George S. Patton, perhaps the most famous American armored officer, scans the North African desert for signs of enemy activity in 1943. Patton wears the armored force jacket and has added epaulets for rank insignia. Field grade officers and above frequently modified their jackets in the same way. Patton has also affixed his rank insignia to the front of his helmet. Rank would often simply be painted on the front of the helmet. (Ethell Collection)

bove: Two M5 Stuart light tanks cross a small stone bridge. nable to go toe to toe with German armor, for much of the ar the Stuart was used as a reconnaissance vehicle. The nk had a crew of four men and was armed with a 37 mm n. (Ethell Collection)

Below: Sherman tanks outfitted with flamethrowers are used to destroy captured aircraft at Sasebo, Japan, after the Japanese surrender. The flamethrower-equipped Shermans had proven to be very effective in the island-hopping campaigns of the Pacific and were often referred to by the G.I.s as 'Ronson' tanks. (Ethell Collection)

Above: Mines were among the armored soldier's deadliest enemies. Here, a Sherman tank from the 25th Armored Engineer Battalion, fitted out with a T1E3 (M1) mine exploder, clears a road in France. The massive wheels at the front of the tank were designed to set off any mines before they could destroy the vehicle itself. The whole apparatus was so heavy that it frequently required two vehicles to move it forward. (Ethell Collection)

Opposite page top: An armored officer in the tropical worsted wool service coat with khaki cotton shirt and service cap. This uniform was similar to the standard green officers' service jacket, but did not feature a belt at the waist.

He wears his armored division patch on his right sleeve, indicating previous service in that unit. Just visible on his left shoulder is the red and green *fourragère* for the Belgian *croix de guerre*.

Right: Two crewmen in Vietnam examine their tank. Both are wearing the jungle uniform. The main armament on this M728 (the combat engineer variant of the M60 tank) is a 165 mm demolition gun. Although no armor versus armor battles took place between North Vietnamese and American forces in Vietnam, armored vehicles proved useful as protection for road convoys and as bulldozers.

Above left: Tanks require almost constant maintenance. In Vietnam, a crewman of an M48 medium tank works to fix a broken track. He is wearing the third model of rip-stop jungle fatigue uniform and tropical combat boots. As was common for troops on operations, his jacket is free of name tape and U.S. Army tape. Just visible on his upturned collar are the clasps for holding his pinned-on, subdued, collar insignia.

Left: An M551 Sheridan tank advancing on the enemy. The Sheridan had been designed originally as a light tank that could be used by airborne divisions to provide armored support. Its relatively small size proved ideal in the jungle conditions of Vietnam. Here, the crew have rigged up a chain-link 'curtain' to the front of the tank to help guard against enemy rocket attacks. The crewmen are wearing the standard M1 helmet with camouflage cover and M1956 flak vest.

Above: While armored forces had not played a very large role in Vietnam, the United States did maintain large armored forces in Europe throughout the Cold War. Here, two M60 tanks take part in exercises in Germany. The tanks have been painted in a light and dark brown camouflage pattern. The crew are wearing the combat vehicle crewman's helmet and the M1965 cold weather field coat. The M1965 field coat was an improved version of the earlier M1943 and M1951 field jacket.

Right: Two crewmen of an M48 tank stay alert as they advance through thick foliage. They are wearing the M1 helmet with camouflage helmet cover and the green cateen fatigue uniform. Both have been able to obtain headsets for their microphone and receivers, allowing them to continue to wear the M1 helmet. Unlike the armored crewman's helmet worn during World War II and Korea, the Cold War era version could not be worn with the M1 helmet.

Left: Three Abrams crewmen inside a tank simulator. They are all wearing combat vehicle crewman's coveralls. Unlike the earlier HBT coverall, this is manufactured from the fire-retardant man-made fabric Nomex.

Below: The participants in the training exercise are debriefed by one of the referees. The men are wearing a combination of the combat crewman's coverall and the standard issue woodland camouflage pattern battle dress uniform (BDU). The BDU is the most commonly worn uniform in the military today.

Above: The United States Army has a long association with the horse. Many of the traditions of the modern armored force began with the horse cavalry, and some of its greatest commanders began their careers as cavalrymen. The army maintained mounted units until the beginning of World War I. Here, cavalrymen take part in a training exercise.

Below: In March 1917, a combined force of horse cavalry and armored car-mounted soldiers take part in a military review in El Paso, Texas. By the turn of the century, the army had begun to experiment with how the horse could work with the internal combustion engine. The cavalrymen and the soldiers in armored cars are all wearing the M1912 olive drab uniform with campaign hat and canvas leggings. The cords on the campaign hat were yellow – the branch color for the cavalry.

Above: Other early experiments with mechanization included mounting artillery pieces on tractors. Here, in 1917, officers examine an early 'self-propelled' 75 mm gun in tests against a comparable horse-drawn artillery piece. The men in the picture are all wearing the olive drab service uniform and campaign hat. The two men standing second and third from the right are wearing the officers' short mackinaw coat.

Below: One officer who developed an early interest in the potential of armored warfare was George S. Patton, who would go on to command the first successful American armored assault of World War I. Here Patton, still a lieutenant colonel, is wearing the officers' olive drab coat with breeches and overseas cap. This uniform resembled th enlisted M1912 uniform but was generally cut from finer material. Patton is standing in front of a French-built Renault tank.

Right: Two members of Patton's command prepare their Renault for action. Both men are wearing the standard M1912 olive drab uniform with leggings and a leather jerkin. The jerkin, adopted from the British, was found to be really suited for wear by the doughboys in the cramped quarters of the early tanks. The soldier standing outside the tank is wearing the standard dishpan helmet and has a box respirator slung over his shoulder.

Below: An officer stands between two of his Renault tanks during World War I. The man on the far left wears a two-piece fatigue uniform, the one on the far right a one-piece uniform. At the beginning of the war, fatigue uniforms were constructed of a light brown canvas; this was later changed to blue denim. The officer is wearing the wool officers' uniform with the leggings and Sam Browne belt popular with European officers.

Right: On the morning of 29 August 1918, French Renault tanks move up to support operations near Juvigny, France. The Renault was the tank most frequently used by the Americans during the war. It was armed with a Hotchkiss machine gun and could travel at the rate of 5.5 miles an hour. Despite its light armament and slowness, the Renault was instrumental in the development of the American armored force.

Below: The crew of an M2A3 light tank during the 1930s. The M2 was widely used by the army in the years before World War II. Its twin turrets featured a .50 caliber machine gun and a .30 caliber machine gun. Its light armor made it wholly unsuited to the modern battlefield, but it was useful in training future armored leaders. This picture was taken as the army was beginning to develop specialized clothing and equipment for its armored forces. While these men are all wearing an early version of the armored helmet, three of them are wearing the mackinaw coat issued to all vehicle crewmen, and the man on the left is wearing a privately acquired leather jacket.

Right: A close-up view of the driver and gunner's compartment on the M2 tank. These relatively open compartments would allow both men to escape quickly, but would offer little protection from enemy ordnance. The many sharp angles on this tank also illustrate the importance of providing tank crew with some sort of protective helmet.

Left: During a maneuve prior to Pearl Harbor, armored crewmen conf with reconnaissance m in their White scout ca The two tankers kneeli at the front are wearing the armored forces cre helmet. Of special interest is the first model tankers' jacket being worn by the offic standing second from the left. Barely visible i the picture, his coat features two patch pockets at the front of the jacket. Later, and more common, models featured slash pockets. Also of interest is the mounted forces holster being worn by the soldier squatting on th far left.

Left: At the start of the war, the United States found itself woefully short of modern weapons. Here, the dummy tank 'Dry Run' is placed over the top of a jeep for training purposes. The man on the far left is wearing one-piece HBT coveralls, the man in the center the first model two-piece HBT fatigue uniform. Both of these men are wearing the HBT 'Daisy Mae' fatigue hat. The jeep driver is wearing the khaki cotton service shirt.

Left: M2A4 light tanks take part in a ceremony marking the opening of Patterson and Meeks Airfields, Keflavik, Iceland, in March 1943. The tank commanders are all wearing the earlier model of armored forces helmet, with rubber ring on the outside of the helmet, which they are wearing over the winter combat helmet.

Below: General George S. Patton (left) talks with another officer during maneuvers. He is wearing the first pattern Parsons field jacket, featuring closed pocket flaps, and a first model *papier mâché* helmet liner. Of special interest is the 2d Armored Division insignia which he has sewn over his left breast. Patton had originally ordered this to be done by all members of the division to improve morale. It became a popular method of wearing the patch, and was taken up throughout World War II by maNy members of other armored units.

Above: Before the war, Patton was one of the tank's main proponents. He has added shoulder epaulets to his HBT coverall uniform to display rank. He is wearing the early armored forces helmet without rigid ear flaps or internal radio headset.

Left: Creighton Abrams was also a pioneer in armored warfare. Pictured here in February 1937 as a young second lieutenant of cavalry, Abrams went on to achieve fame during World War II when he served with the 4th Armored Division. After the war he rose to command American forces in Vietnam, and retired as chief of staff of the army. In this picture, Abrams is wearing the Model 1926 olive drab officers' service coat, with the crossed swords of the cavalry on his lapels, and the M1921 officers' Sam Browne sword belt over his coat.

Right: A group of officers from the 1st Armored Division land in Sicily in July 1943. All of these men are wearing the wool service shirt with M1 helmets. The MP standing second from the right has the 1st Armored Division shoulder patch sewn to his left shoulder above his MP brassard. The brassard was secured by a safety pin and could be removed. The captain standing at the center is wearing the officers' wool service shirt, distinguished by the shoulder epaulets. The general third from the left is wearing a winter combat jacket, its wool-knit collar turned down to reveal his rank insignia. The general fourth from the left wears the dark-shade winter shirt more commonly seen worn with the winter service uniform.

ight: Produced in
uantity until March
41, the M3 light
nk was the best the
nited States had at
e beginning of World
ar II. It featured a
veted hull and seven-
ded turret, and was
med with a 37 mm
un and two .30
liber machine guns.
rmor's roots in the
valry arm can be
en by the crossed
words of this
connaissance tank.

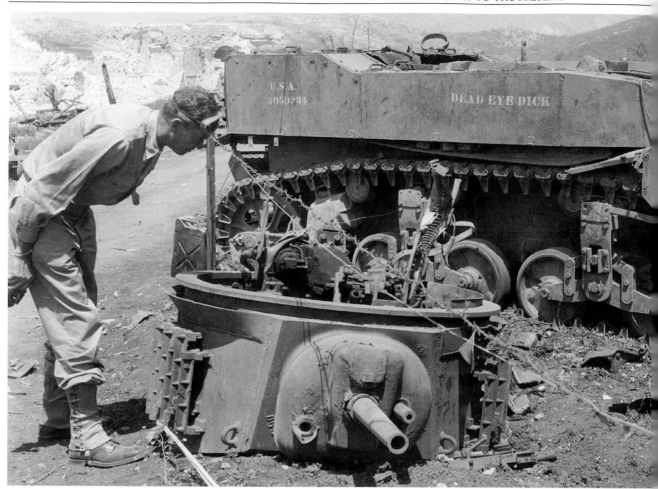

Left: An American officer examines the remains of 'Dead Eye Dick', an M5 tank destroyed in the battles around Cassino, Italy. The officer is wearing the khaki cotton summer uniform, service shoes and leggings. His shirt is an officers' pattern with shoulder epaulets; his trousers, with pocket flaps on the hip pockets, are also officers' pattern. The khaki service uniform was not often worn under combat conditions in Europe.

Opposite page, bottom: Early in 1941, M3 light tanks halt in a shallow river-bed. The early models of the M3 light tank, pictured here, featured an entirely riveted construction. Behind the foremost M3 is an M2 medium tank, the precursor of the M3 and M4. All of the crewmen are wearing the early pattern armored forces helmet and HBT coveralls. Also of interest are the early M1917A1 dishpan helmets and khaki service uniforms being worn by the men in the early MA model jeep.

Below: M4 and M4A1 Sherman tanks, operating in support of the 34th Infantry Division, enter Livorno, Italy in July 1944. The M4 series of Sherman tanks were the work horses of the American armored forces throughout World War II. Although often outclassed by their larger German opponents, the Sherman tank proved to be an easily manufactured, versatile and reliable tank. The M4 at the left of the picture has additional armor welded to its side to provide further protection to the ammunition stowage areas.

Left: M4 Sherman tanks unload from LS 77 on the Anzio, Italy waterfront in 1944. The LST could transport vehicles and men virtually anywhere, and saw extensive service during amphibious operations throughout the war. The crews of these Sherman tanks have added extra sections of track to the front of their tanks to improve their protection. The commander of the first tank has chosen to wear the standard M1 helmet in lieu of the armored forces crew helmet.

Above: General Patton observes a training maneuver in England prior to the invasion of France. Patton is wearing an officers' field overcoat and M1 helmet. The crew of the tank are wearing herringbone twill fatigue uniforms with leggings, and the crewman sitting on the tank is wearing the armored forces helmet. Patton assumed command of the 3d Army shortly after the Allies landed in France. His dynamic use of armor would make the 3d Army one of the most successful, and famous, American armies of the war.

Left: Sherman tanks of the 755th tank battalion provide fire-support to advancing infantry troops in Pietramala, Italy in 1944. The ability of tanks to keep up with advancing infantry in the hilly terrain meant that they were often utilized in Italy as 'mobile artillery'. Independent tank battalions, such as the 755th, were often attached to infantry units in a supporting role.

Left: This Sherman tank has had special hedgerow-busting teeth welded to the front of the tank. These devices were designed by Sergeant Curtis G. Culin of the 102d Cavalry Reconnaissance Squadron. They were improvised from German beach defenses along the Normandy coast, and allowed Allied armor to plow through hedgerows instead of trying to go over the top of them. This innovation was so important to Allied success in Normandy that Culin was later awarded the Legion of Merit.

Left: Private Walter Hatfield has dismounted from his tank 'Hun Chaser' to search for the enemy amid the ruins of St Lo, France, in July 1944. Like their counterparts in the Army Air Corps, tank crewmen often gave names to their vehicles. Private Hatfield is wearing the wool service uniform with his tankers' helmet, and is armed with an M1911A1 .45 caliber automatic pistol.

Above: M18 mechanics pose for the camera. They are wearing HBT fatigue jackets and trousers. The man on the right is wearing the second pattern HBT trousers with patch pockets on the thighs, and a leather garrison belt. He is holding an oiler, to be found in every vehicle's tool kit.

Left: During the 3d Army's 1944 race across France, Major General Wood, the commander of the 4th Armored Division, confers with members of his staff. He is wearing the winter combat jacket, to which he has added epaulets. Reminiscent of the cavalry, he is wearing riding boots and breeches. Wood was one of General Patton's most aggressive and able armored commanders. In December 1944, the 4th Armored Division would be the first armored formation to reach the besieged defenders of Bastogne.

Below: Tanks provide transportation for infantrymen of the 35th Infantry Division in January 1945. These tanks have been whitewashed to provide camouflage. Tanks would often be employed as personnel carriers. The commander of the tank in the foreground has bundled himself up with the winter combat helmet and enlisted pattern overcoat with upturned collar. He is almost indistinguishable from the infantrymen riding on his tank.

Above: A Sherman tank of the 3d Armored Division provides transportation for soldiers of the 9th Infantry Division as they advance through the Siegfried Line in September 1944. Visible to the left of the tank are concrete 'dragons' teeth', designed to prevent tanks from advancing. Also of interest is the bulldozer plow that has been attached to the front of the vehicle, the connecting arm of which is just visible on the wheels of the tank. The number of infantrymen riding on this Sherman, and the open commander's hatch, would indicate that the enemy is not nearby.

Opposite page, top: Tanks of the 20th Armored Division prepare to continue their advance through Munich. The Allied star has been painted on the turret of the tank at the front of the column to identify the tank to Allied planes. Leading the advance into the city is a jeep, known to armored soldiers as a 'peep'. The crew of this peep have added a cutter bar to the front bumper to cut the wires that were strung across roads by retreating German soldiers.

Opposite page, bottom: Tanks of the 7th Armored Division' 40th Tank Battalion fire on German positions during the Battle of the Bulge. The 7th Armored Division was heavily involved in the battles around St Vith, Belgium. These tanks have all been painted white in an effort to blend in with their surroundings. The crewmen of the tank on the left are wearing M1938 enlisted overcoats to provide additional warmth.

pposite page, top: Sherman tanks of the 2d Armored ivision advance through a German town. The crew of this nk have secured sandbags, held in place with chicken wire, the sides of their tank for additional protection from erman anti-tank weapons. Just visible on the right front of e tank is the designation for the 67th Armored Battalion, l Armored Division. Such identification was often eliberately obscured or removed during operations in the eld.

pposite page, bottom: M5A1 light tanks of the 2d Armored ivision move through a European town. The tanks are estooned with a variety of personal equipment designed to ake their crews more comfortable. The tank at the rear of the column carries logs on its side, which would provide additional protection to the crews and would be used as traction for tanks stuck in the mud. The crewmen of these vehicles have opted to wear the M1 helmet instead of the armored forces helmet.

Below: An M4A3 Sherman tank, the final Sherman variant of the war, advancing through the remains of a German town. This upgunned Sherman, christened 'Elsie' by her crew, is armed with a 76 mm gun which provided additional fire power. The larger gun required that the turret of the tank be redesigned. Elsie's crew have decided to use the tank's .50 caliber machine gun stowing rack to carry additional equipment, a common practice.

Left: In 1947, veterans of a National Guard armored unit that had been mobilized in 1941 are gathered together for a reunion. The men are wearing a combination of M1939 wool service jackets and shorter 'Ike' jackets, peaked caps and overseas caps. Visible on the left shoulders of many of these men is the triangle patch of the armored forces, while many have service chevrons on their left sleeves, indicating long service overseas.

Above: Crewmen of the 66th Armored Regiment, 2d Armored Division, are reviewed at the end of the war. The men are all wearing short wool service jackets and trousers, two-buckle service boots and M1 steel helmets. The flag at the right of the picture is the guidon for Company E of the 66th Armored Regiment, and features the silhouette of a World War I British heavy tank, used as the branch symbol of the armored force.

Left: Although tanks were not as frequently used in the Pacific, some Sherman tanks were used to great effect against Japanese fortifications. Here, tanks of the 175th Tank Battalion advance on Baguio, Luzon, in the Philippines. The crewmen of these tanks have adorned them with a variety of artwork, and have added additional track to the turrets.

Above: American tanks transport South Korean soldiers during the Korean War. These tanks are flying Confederate battle flags from their radio antennas for identification and as a means of improving *esprit de corps*. The tank in the foreground carries additional ammunition for its .50 caliber machine gun in cans resting on a shelf at the back of the tank.

Opposite page, bottom: An M26 Pershing heavy tank crew in Korea. The crew have painted this tank with a tiger's face, as it was believed that communist Chinese soldiers were frightened of tigers. Many American tanks in Korea featured similar artwork, most notably Rice's Red Devils. These crewmen are all wearing the cotton field jacket. The two men in the rear of the picture are wearing the M1951 pile cap.

Right: An M4A3E8 Sherman tank in Korea, being used as an engineer vehicle. Just visible at the front of the tank is a dozer-blade. On the side of the turret the crew has painted the tank's name, and to the right of this has been stenciled a castle, the branch insignia for engineers. The crew of 'Pine Mt.' have chosen to equip their tank with an additional .30 caliber machine gun, which is on the turret next to the tank's .50 caliber machine gun.

Above: Tanks of the 70th Tank Battalion support the advance of men of the 1st Cavalry Division, serving as an infantry unit, as they assault a hill north of Wanggok, Korea. These crewmen are wearing the cotton field uniform and pile cap.

Opposite page, top: Supreme Court Justice Raymond Givens is given a ride in an M24 light tank. The tank crewmen are wearing cotton field jackets with M5 protective helmets. This helmet was originally designed to be worn by aircraft crews with their flak armor during World War II, but it was found that, with the ear pieces removed, the M5 was well suited for use by armored crews.

Right: M24 crewmen with a dignitary. The crewmen are all wearing HBT fatigue uniforms. The tank commander has a T45 microphone, which allowed him to communicate with the rest of his crew while keeping his hands free. It was designed during World War II.

Opposite page, top: Tank crewmen inspect an M24 light tank. They are wearing third pattern HBT utility uniform and two-buckle service shoes left over from World War II. So much material had been produced for use during the war that much of it could be seen in use throughout the 1950s. The men are all wearing the armored forces insignia on their left breast. Also of interest are the smaller NCO stripes being worn. These proved to be very unpopular, and were not used after the war in Korea.

Opposite page, bottom: An M4A3 tank crew of the 106th Tank Battalion during a 1952 training exercise. They are wearing World War II surplus HBT fatigue uniforms. Three of the crewmen are wearing M1 helmet liners, and the driver is wearing a cotton field cap. Visible on the inside of the driver's hatch is the periscope that allows the driver to see while the tank is 'buttoned up' with all of its hatches closed.

Above: While the army found itself engaged against hostile forces in Korea, it still had to keep forces in Europe to guard against a possible Soviet offensive. Here, a Pershing heavy tank patrols the border between East and West Germany. The tank commander is wearing an armored forces helmet and herringbone uniform. To the outside of the turret the crew has secured an M1943 field pack. This field gear had been introduced at the end of World War II, but did not see widespread use until the Korean War.

Left: A Sherman tank crew prepare for field exercises wearing M48 cold weather parkas. These were part of the cold weather clothing system that featured several layers of cotton clothing designed to provide added warmth to soldiers operating in the field.

Right: Crewmen of the 644th Tank Battalion arrive for training at Camp Drum, New York. They are wearing a combination of HBT and cotton sateen fatigue clothing, together with the blocked field cap that became popular during the Korean War. The soldier at the front is carrying B Company's guidon, the later pattern that featured the silhouette of a Pershing tank and crossed swords. He is wearing a shoulder holster for his M1911 A1 pistol.

Right: A Pershing tank crossing a recently completed bridge during a training exercise in the late 1950s. All of the tank crewmen are wearing World War II vintage armored forces helmets. The sergeant on the left is wearing herringbone twill fatigue clothing with combat service boots. These boots were similar to those worn by paratroopers, but did not feature the beveled heel found on jump boots.

Opposite page: M48s nearing completion at a Chrysler production facility. The M48 was the standard American medium tank throughout the late 1950s and the 1960s. It would become the army's principal tank during the Vietnam War.

Right: An armored crewman in Vietnam works on his .50 caliber machine gun. This crewman is wearing a M1952 fragmentation flak vest. Visible in front of his machine gun are two combat vehicle crewman helmets. Unlike the earlier armored forces helmet that had been worn throughout World War II and Korea, the combat vehicle crewman's helmet did provide the wearer with some ballistic protection.

Below: An M48A3 tank operating in Vietnam. The crew of this tank have attached several boxes of C rations and some duffel-bags to bustle racks on the back of the turret. The commander of this tank has chosen to wear the standard M1 helmet with camouflage helmet cover instead of the vehicle crewman's helmet.

Sergeant Sammy Davis wears the army green service uniform. This uniform was introduced in the late 1950s, and replaced the earlier olive drab shade 33 field jacket that had been introduced at the end of World War II. The green service uniform remains in use today. Sergeant Davis wears the 2d Armored Division patch on his left shoulder. This version features the unit's nickname 'Hell on Wheels' on a tab below the patch. His branch of service disc is that of the Air Defense Artillery. The green loops on his shoulder straps indicate a combat leader. Sergeant Davis received the Medal of Honor during the Vietnam War.

Above: General Creighton Abrams reviews Army of the Republic of Vietnam (ARVN) soldiers in 1968. Abrams, who gained fame during his service with the 4th Armored Division in World War II, later became commander of all American forces in Vietnam. He is wearing the third pattern tropical combat uniform with subdued insignia. By 1968, this was standard uniform amongst all combat soldiers in Vietnam.

Below: Tanks of the 1st Cavalry Division take part in a review. The crewmen are all wearing the combat vehicle crewman's helmet. They are also wearing rayon cravats in yellow, their branch color. Also of interest are the infra-red searchlight covers on the turrets of their tanks, featuring a black horse head on a yellow field.

Above: Two officers confer on the back of an M48 tank during training maneuvers in 1967. The two generals are wearing green sateen utility uniforms with utility caps and black leather combat boots. The officer on the right wears the second pattern utility uniform, which featured clip corners on the pockets, and the black leather general officers' pistol belt. The officer on the left is wearing the standard web pistol belt with black leather .45 holster. Both men are wearing full color insignia on their fatigue uniforms.

Opposite page, top: An M48 Tank during maneuvers in Germany. The crewmen are both wearing the combat vehicle crewman's helmet. The commander is wearing the M1965 field jacket. This tank does not feature the field modifications that would be found on tanks operating in the war zone.

Right: Major General George S. Patton, Jr., the commander of the 2d Armored Division, during a training exercise at Fort Hood, Texas, in 1976. General Patton wears the green sateen utility uniform with subdued insignia. Just visible over his left breast is the subdued patch of the 2d Armored Division. Wearing the patch over the left breast was a practice begun by Patton's father when he founded the division.

Right: Tanks of B company, 377th Armored Battalion, during reinforcement of forces exercises in Germany (REFORGER) in 1984, taking up positions outside Itzlingen, Germany. The crewmen are all wearing M1965 field jackets and DH132 armored vehicle crewman's helmets, which are an improved version of the helmet that was worn during Vietnam.

Below: An M60A1 tank during training maneuvers. The M60 replaced the M48 and was America's main battle tank throughout the 1970s and 1980s. The tanker in this picture is wearing the DH132 armored vehicle crewman's helmet.

Opposite page, right: Early in the 1980s, a tank crew prepare to exchange their M60A3 tank (left) for a new M1A1 Abrams main battle tank. The men are wearing combat vehicle crewman coveralls and high temperature-resistant, cold weather jackets. The vehicle crewman's clothing is constructed of a special fire-retardant fabric. The Abrams tank was named in honor of Creighton Abrams and is now the main battle tank of all U.S. armored forces.

Opposite page, top: A tank of 221st Cavalry Regiment aims its gun on the move. The extraordinarily sophisticated Abrams tank allows the crew to level, aim and fire its 120mm guns at speeds in excess of fifty miles per hour. This tank also has an M2 .50 caliber machine gun and a 7.62 mm machine gun on the turret.

Above: Abrams mechanics work on a tank during exercises at Fort Irwin, California, in 1995. These men are wearing the second pattern desert BDU, which featured only light tones. This uniform was not issued until after the Persian Gulf War.

Left: During the Persian Gulf War, the crew of an Abrams tank compare their vehicle to a recently captured, Russian-built T72 Iraqi tank. This crew is wearing a combination of the woodland pattern and the desert pattern BDUs. The soldier on the left is wearing the tan 'chocolate chip' uniform. The remainder of the crew are wearing woodland pattern camouflage. America's deployment to the Persian Gulf was so rapid that many of the soldiers deployed were not able to receive desert camouflage uniforms.

Above: Close up view of the DH132 armored vehicle crewman's helmet, which consists of an outer protective shell attached to a separate mesh inner liner. It combines the features of previous armored helmets, and provides the vehicle crewman with both ballistic and crash protection.

Opposite page, top: A mechanic works on the back of an Abrams tank. He is wearing woodland pattern BDU and black leather combat boots. BDUs are the standard service uniform of all branches of the United States military.

Below: M60 tank crewmen confer over a map during a REFORGER exercise in 1985. Both men are wearing DH132s. The tanker on the left is wearing an insulated helmet liner under his helmet. Both men are wearing olive drab wet weather parkas.

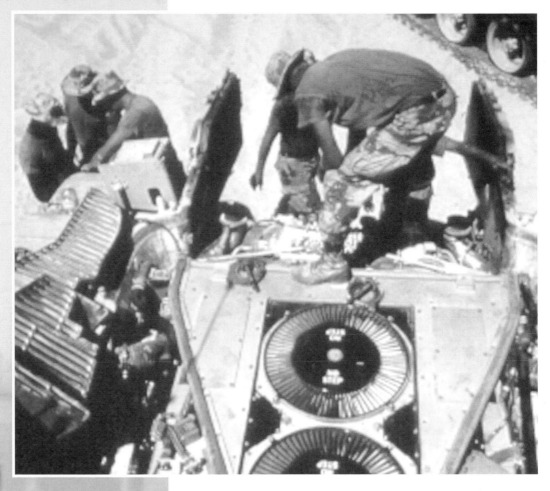

Above: M60 tank mechanics perform repairs on a tank during Operation Bright Star. They are all wearing OG107 T-shirts, desert daytime camouflage trousers and boonie hats, together with standard issue black leather combat boots.

Left: A 3d Armored Division tank during a Reforger exercise in Germany in 1985. The two crew members are wearing DH132 helmets with M1944 wind and dust goggles and olive drab extreme cold weather parkas.

Left: A tank gunner aims his gun. He is wearing green sateen fatigue uniform with a subdued armored forces patch on the left shoulder. Despite the many advances that have been made in tank design since World War I, the inside of a modern main battle tank is still cramped and uncomfortable.

Right: An M551 crewman on look-out in the commander's cupola. This picture shows some of the variety of personal equipment that vehicle crewmen may attach to their tanks to improve comfort. Visible on this tank are several collapsible cots and a medium combat field pack.

Left: A vehicle commander receiving instructions on the headset of his DH132 helmet. He is wearing issue aviator's sunglasses and woodland pattern BDU jacket. He is also wearing a shoulder harness for the all-purpose lightweight individual carrying equipment (ALICE). He has attached a privately acquired knife to the left shoulder of his harness equipment.

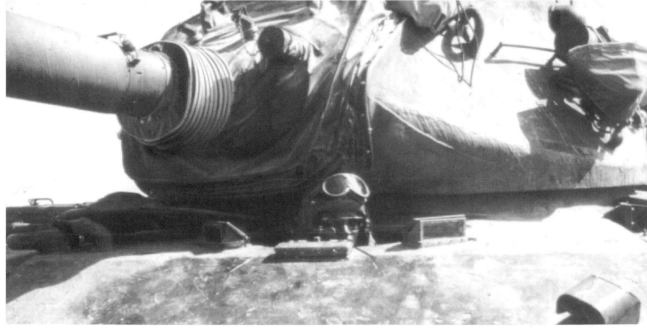

Opposite page, top: A tank crewman works on tightening the wheels of his tank during a desert operation. He is wearing the olive T-shirt with first pattern desert daytime camouflage trousers and 'Boonie' hat.

Opposite page, bottom: Although the Abrams tank was the principal American tank of the Persian Gulf War, some M60A3 tanks were also used. The driver of this M60A3 is keeping a watch on the area around his tank. In addition to his dust goggles, he is also wearing a pair of sunglasses to fight the glare.

Above: The commander of an M60 tank directs the advance of his squadron's tanks. The crew members are wearing the Vietnam-era helmet and the M65 cotton field jacket. The unit crest for the 32d Armored Regiment, 3d Armored Division, is painted on the side of the turret. Also of interest is the Playboy bunny symbol painted on the side of the tank's gun barrel.

Opposite page, top: An M551 tank crew on patrol in the desert. This vehicle is carrying a large amount of personal equipment. Of special interest is the tape over the muzzle of the tank's gun, a precaution necessitated by the dusty conditions encountered in the desert.

Above: Vehicle crewmen loading ammunition for their Abrams 120 mm gun into their tank. They are all wearing the desert fatigue uniform. Because of fear of an Iraqi chemical attack, these men are wearing the M10A1 masks that are issued to armored crewmen. Unlike the infantry soldiers' M17A2 mask, which has its own filters, the M10A1 uses filters found inside the tank.

Left: The crew of an M1 Abrams tank take care of some housekeeping in the Saudi Arabian Desert. Both men are wearing the first pattern daytime desert camouflage uniform. The man on the left has painted the outer shell of his DH132 helmet in tan. The soldier on the right wears the desert 'Boonie' hat.

Below: An M551 tank crewman of the 82d Airborne Division in Saudi Arabia. Only the tanker on the far right of the picture is wearing the full desert camouflage uniform. The rest of the men are wearing vehicle crewman coveralls. All of the tankers are wearing the Personnel Armor System Groun Troops (PASGT) helmet, more commonly known as the 'fritz helmet, with desert camouflage cover; and nylon ALICE loac bearing equipment.

Left: After arriving in Saudi Arabia, this Abrams tank is being loaded on a flatbed truck for movement further inland. Just visible under the turret is the vehicle's driver. Visible on the side of the tank and the rear of the turret is a unit identification that was frequently seen during the Persian Gulf War.

Top: A vehicle maintenance crew sent to repair an Abrams tank that has thrown a track. The three crewmen on the left are wearing the OG106 mechanics' coverall, while the man standing on the right wears the combat vehicle crewman coverall. The mechanics' coveralls are made in a green sateen material and are intended as a fatigue uniform. They have no fire-retardant qualities.

Above: 82d Airborne trooper, PFC Kocsis, relaxes on the turret of his M551 Sheridan tank, 'Damn Yankee'. It was very common for armored crewmen in Saudi Arabia to name their tanks. Kocsis wears the desert camouflage uniform with green and black subdued insignia, together with privately acquired jungle boots.

Above: M551 Sheridan tanks of the 82d Airborne Division are off-loaded from trucks in Saudi Arabia. The tank, 'Alice Destroyer', has already been off-loaded and festooned with a variety of personal equipment. The crewman in front of Alice Destroyer wears the OG T-shirt and has loosened the top of his vehicle crewman's coverall.

Left: Sheridan tanks lined up before moving out on patrol. The box located above the guns on these tanks is for a thermal sight. All of the tanks of this unit have nicknames beginning with D, indicating that there was a unit policy on the naming of vehicles. The crewmen are wearing a combination of BDUs and coveralls.

Above: Crewmen of the 72d Engineers prepare to test their recently installed mine-clearing rakes. While the rakes have been painted in desert sand color, the vehicles retain the green woodland color. This would indicate that the mine-clearing rakes were not added until after the vehicles had arrived in Saudi Arabia.

Below: Colonel Zanini of the 1st Armored Division briefs his men before a mission. The 1st deployed so rapidly from their base in Bamberg, Germany, that these men have yet to receive desert camouflage uniform. They are wearing either the woodland pattern BDU uniform or wet weather parkas. All of the men are wearing kevlar helmets and ALICE equipment.

Above: A soldier wearing the armored crewman coverall standing on top of Alice Destroyer. Visible to the crewman's left is a plastic five-gallon water can. This model was inspired by the jerry can of World War II fame.

Opposite page: Two M551 crewmen discuss the day's events. They are wearing the desert camouflage uniform and kevlar helmet with desert cover. The soldier with his back to the camera is wearing a basic ALICE rig with two canteens attached to the belt. Just visible on the back of his helmet are two squares of reflective material.

Left: An M60A3 tanker aims his vehicle's gun during operations in Saudi Arabia. He is wearing desert uniform with the sleeves rolled up, and a DH132 helmet that has been painted in a sand color. The picture illustrates the cramped conditions found inside the M60 tank.

Above: At the conclusion of an operation in the field, these tank crewmen are scouring their Abrams tanks with high pressure hoses. They are all wearing wet weather parkas and trousers with camouflage combat caps.

Below: During a training operation at Fort Lewis, Washington an M1A1 Abrams tank supports some nearby infantrymen. The tank has a white unit designation on its left side. Such designations originated during the Persian Gulf War, when they were used for the easy identification of Allied vehicles.